spot

HOLIDAYS

RAMADAN

by Mari Schuh

AMICUS | AMICUS INK

Quran

rug

Look for these words and pictures as you read.

food

dates

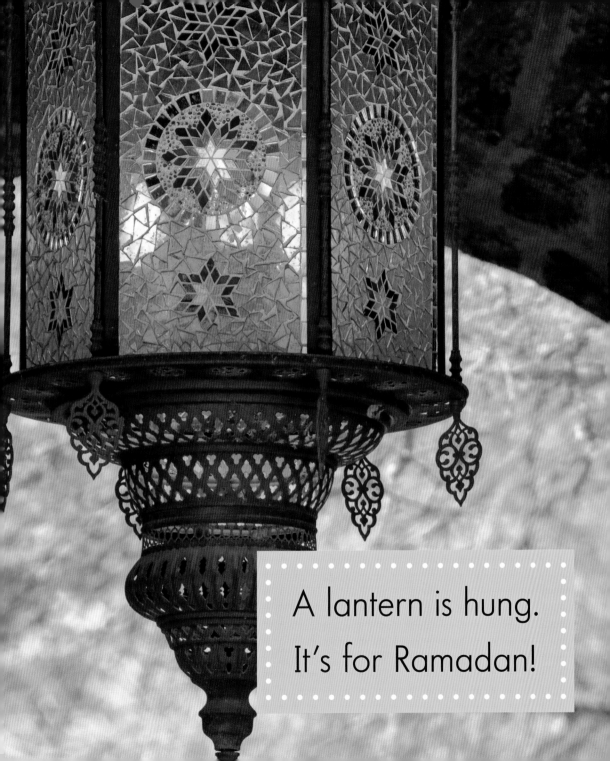

A lantern is hung.
It's for Ramadan!

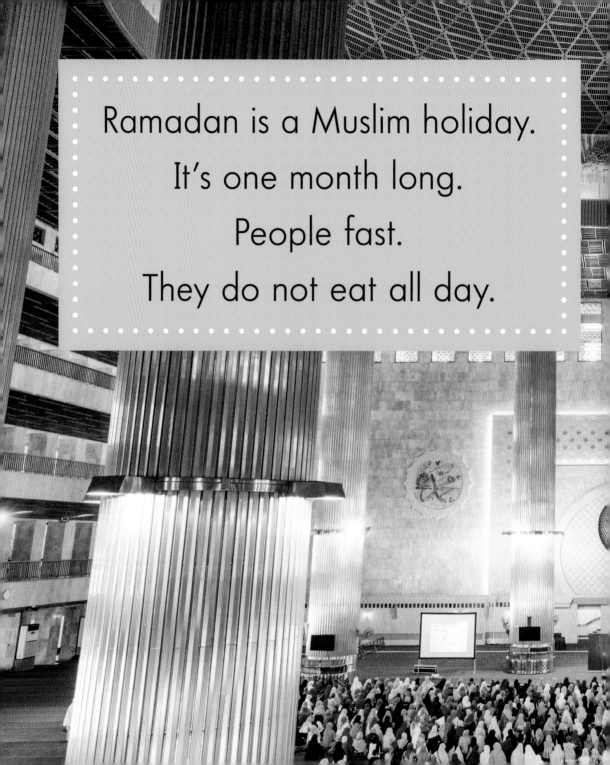

Ramadan is a Muslim holiday.
It's one month long.
People fast.
They do not eat all day.

Quran

See the Quran?

It's a holy book.

It's used to pray.

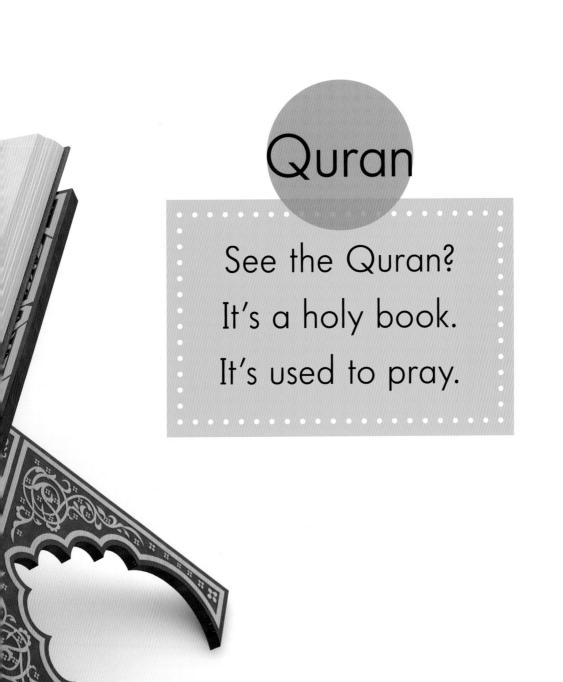

See the rug?
People pray on it.

rug

food

See the food?
The sun has set.
It's time to eat!

See the dates?
They are a sweet fruit.
They are a snack after dark.

dates

A boy prays.
People help others.
It's a holy month.

See the Quran?
It's a holy book.
It's used to pray.

See the rug?
People pray on it.

rug

Quran

rug

Did you find?

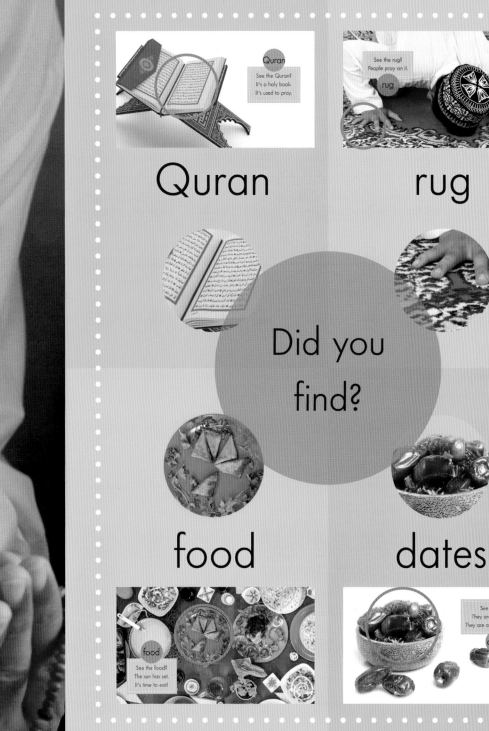

food

dates

food

See the food?
The sun has set.
It's time to eat!

See the dates?
They are a sweet fruit.
They are a snack after dark.

dates

Spot is published by Amicus and Amicus Ink
P.O. Box 1329, Mankato, MN 56002
www.amicuspublishing.us

Library of Congress Cataloging-in-Publication Data
Names: Schuh, Mari C., 1975- author.
Title: Ramadan / by Mari Schuh.
Description: Mankato, MN : Amicus, [2020] | Series:
  Spot holidays
Identifiers: LCCN 2018053525 (print) | LCCN 2018054172
  (ebook) | ISBN 9781681518466 (pdf) | ISBN 9781681518060
  (library binding) | ISBN 9781681525341 (pbk.)
Subjects: LCSH: Ramadan—Juvenile literature. | Fasts and
  feasts—Islam—Juvenile literature.
Classification: LCC BP186.4 (ebook) | LCC BP186.4 .S326 2020
  (print) | DDC 297.3/62—dc23
LC record available at https://lccn.loc.gov/2018053525

Printed in China

HC 10 9 8 7 6 5 4 3 2 1
PB 10 9 8 7 6 5 4 3 2 1

Alissa Thielges, editor
Deb Miner, series designer
Veronica Scott, book designer
Holly Young and Shane Freed,
  photo researchers

Photos by Shutterstock/M Salem cover,
16; Shutterstock/Karrrtinki 1; Alamy/
Naushad Kallivalappil 3; Getty/Nikada
4-5; Getty/saffetucuncu 6-7; Getty/
DistinctiveImages 8-9; Getty/Jasmin
Merdan 10-11; iStock/triocean 12-13;
Shutterstock/Mama Belle and the kids
14-15

RAMADAN